The Little Book of Daytime Illusions

By Kevin James

Everyone is creative. It is only when we tell ourselves we are incapable of creating a beautiful picture that we limit our amazing capabilities.

The Introduction

The Little Book of Daytime Illusions by Kevin James is the result of when one expresses the random ideas and pictures that come through the mind at any given time. The Little Book of Daytime Illusions isn't about careless creations but the **inspired action** a creator must take when suddenly gifted with an idea. Do not be afraid to express your creative abilities and present them for the rest of the world to see. The Little Book of Daytime Illusions will inspire you to do so.

Utilize and enjoy the free space inside of The Little Book of Daytime Illusions to express your own creative ideas. Are you ready to let your mind wander at the wondrous possibilities of the mind? You're in for a treat. The beginning of The Little Book of Daytime Illusions is an excerpt from "The Prosperous Reflection", my first book. Please enjoy.

CREATIVITY,

The Catalyst

Creativity is a mental faculty I have been exercising and developing since a young age, so it will be beneficial for you to give your attention to what comes from the chapter. Creativity is something you develop before the moment you board your first bus or take your first car ride to preschool. As children, we tend to find the most convenient way to express our creativity. You'd get in the car or bus on a chilly August morning with the other kids and blow your breath on the window to begin making either a message or a masterpiece. Your mind begins to unravel at the possibilities of what the day may entail. Who will you meet, what will your teachers be like, what will you learn, what will you begin to discover about yourself? These are the creative questions you will be asking yourself because they will activate scenarios in your mind telling a story of what may occur.

I knew that no matter what, what made me comfortable and serene was expressing my thoughts through my creative faculties. No matter what the day had in store, no matter whom I met, I knew long ago what made me happy as a child. Also, no matter what phase I may have been in from childhood through adolescence, others recognized my skill through what made me happy. I could have been the worst dressed in school, but best artist. Do you see my point? What did people always give you recognition for? What do people give you recognition for now? The recognition you receive for what you naturally love to do is your great creative ability peeking through your character, even if you haven't figured out what it was just yet.

If you have ever paid attention in your surroundings when you were younger to others, it was easy for you to decipher the athletes, the artists, the musicians, the entertainers, and the thinkers before the value and adolescence started to play a role. For example, you knew who the athletes were in school that was passionate about their sport of choice. You could certainly tell what interested others because you would adapt yourself to what interested them in conversation. Adaptation is how you made friends in certain instances. In adulthood, adaptation is how you make potential business partners. When you and another have a common creative pursuit, your progress will develop and you both will develop your skills tremendously. No matter what happens, every experience such as the one discussed will strengthen rather than weaken your creativity.

In life we become bombarded by opinions, suggestions, and orders over time and it becomes easy to lose the inner child who knew who we were all along. You see what's really happening from childhood up into adulthood is we are developing distinctive qualities about ourselves, which we have always possessed. There comes a point in time when we stretch our interests to match that of others and lose track of our own capabilities. Your own creativity will act as a magnet, pulling the people and resources toward you to fuel it even more, trust me. So never worry or fear if there will be interest in you once you pursue your creative endeavors, you will be respected and loved much more for spreading your creativity and talent.

The Imagination

Thinking about our relationship with the Universe and what all it could possibly entail will heighten your creative ability to infinite levels. What happens when you think about your relationship with the Universe is your mind opens up to greater possibilities about yourself and your abilities. You instantly knock down earthly barriers, which would have impeded your progress by looking at them from such a grounded perspective. Imagine your creativity centuries from now; imagine your creativity on other planets, in other galaxies, etc. What do you come up with? You are doing more than opening up new pathways in your creative thinking. You are practicing using one of your greater mental faculties, imagination.

Developing and maintaining creativity from a child-like past time, is as challenging as remembering everything you have learned in elementary, middle, and high school. Creativity comes from the imagination and every day on the second, our imagination grows. With control, the imagination can grow wondrous and magical. Without control, your imagination is going to be working against you rather than for you. You will remain in control of your imagination and your ideas by taking down every idea from the ether you can capture. The key to creativity is your ability to capture the ideas you have from the mind and bring them to life. The idea of thinking of something wonderful and never acting on it is in no way creativity. The idea you may think is stupid may be gold to someone else. Record all of the ideas and thoughts you can, where could it take you?

As adults, the imagination tends to put in overtime, focused solely on "real world" issues, which could directly affect you. When you are working to provide for yourself or your family, most likely you're no longer giving attention to what one would call an" imagination". You're now known as a critical thinker. As an adult, it seems to be more of how can you use the imagination you have left to create more chaos on top of chaos, leaving minimal room for creative, great, positive ideas. When one uses the imagination in a negative manner, they are using the imagination to shape an unfortunate reality of never having or doing enough. The adult who has never learned to make their own decisions, use the power of their mind, and take necessary risks is the same adult who can give you every reason why security is the only way to go. Excuses become dominant in the language of individuals who dare

NOT to use their imagination to bring better results into their lives.

There is a silver lining if you have ever had difficulty accessing the wondrous imagination, believe it or not. All you have to do is lay down one creative brick everyday. Let us use art as an example; being it is a popular medium of expressing creativity. If I wanted to become one of the best artists of my time, I would have to develop my skill everyday. I would develop my skill by devoting 30 minutes to an hour of my time daily to either sketching, painting, organizing my area, writing down a new idea, or gathering materials for my latest work. Realize these are days you aren't getting back and any downtime can easily be transmuted into a profitable product if you let it. The utilization of your time and attention you give to your ideas is what will bring you the best results from that idea.

MATTER CONVERSION.

"The spirit creates
direction from the soul."
...Leland VerVanDen

Crackilye Tree

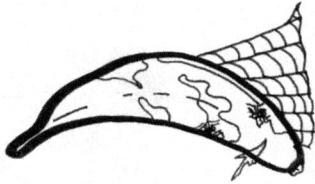

halloween
fruit

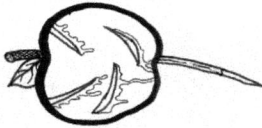

COSMIC *a proper* FALLACY
Discretions

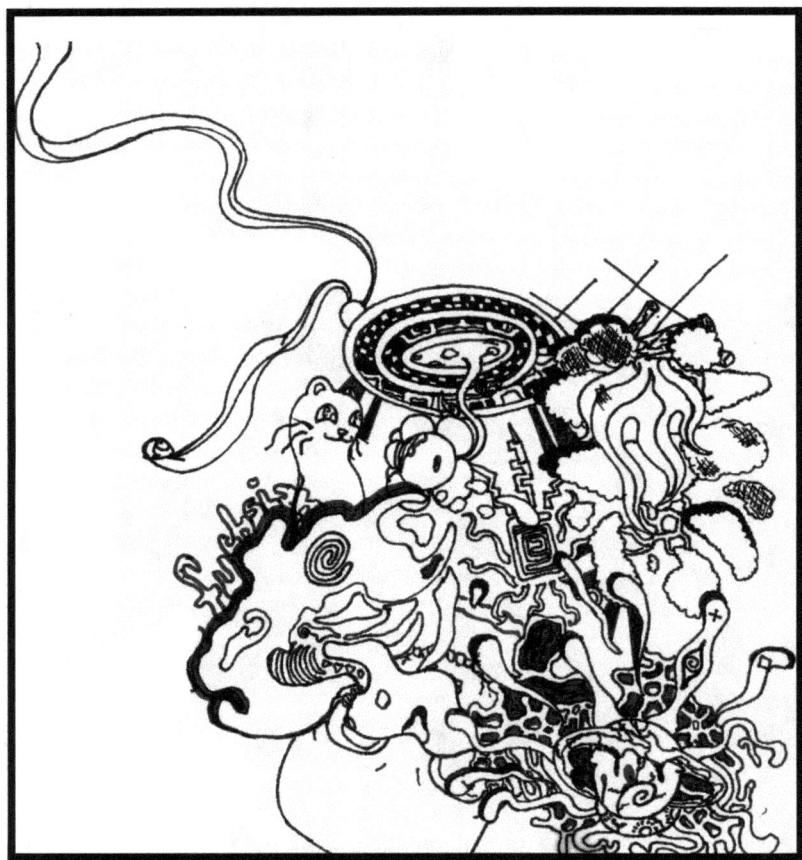

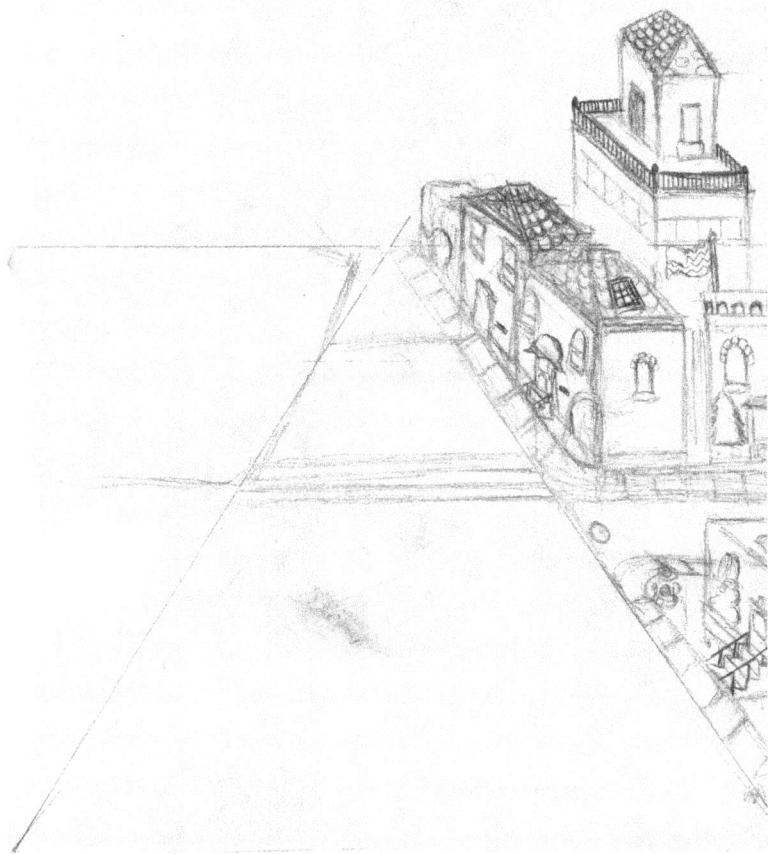

This is the end of The Little Book
of Daytime Illusions by Kevin
James

Perhaps, there will be another.

Visit:

**The Fuchsian Gallery
Company from Kevin James**

thefuchsiangalleryco.com

**The Prosperous Reflection by
Kevin James**

theprosperousreflection.com